The Many Faces of

John McAfee

AN AMERICAN HUSTLER

A 90-Minute Biography

Written by
Steven Matthews

Words Are Swords Publishing

Published in the United States of America by Words Are Swords Publishing, Los Angeles, California.

www.WordsAreSwordsPublishing.com

The Many Faces of John McAfee

First Edition.

THE MANY FACES OF JOHN MCAFEE

Dedicated to a true legend & American hustler,

John McAfee.

May your words of wisdom echo through the ages.

Table of Contents

An Important Message from the Author

Like many aspiring entrepreneurs in the 2000's, I loved watching John McAfee in the headlines. Month after month, John McAfee appeared in a new, shocking headline. It might sound crazy, but watching the man reinvent himself every couple of years gave hope to a lot of people. What other people are saying about you is not written in store and it's never too late to change everything about yourself, just as McAfee did many times.

I put my heart and soul into this book, and before we get to that I have one simple request: Please do not forget to leave a review for this book. The value of book reviews – even just a single review consisting of a few words – can have a tremendous positive impact on the trajectory of books, the people who read them, and the authors who write them.

If you spend the next 30 seconds leaving a review for this book within the marketplace you purchased it, it will not only help *me* enormously, but it will also help readers like you who are looking to be inspired by a mad genius like John McAfee.

Whether you choose to leave a review for this book now or later, by simply sharing one thing you learned or liked about this book in your review you will help support me writing more books like this and more readers around the world who are seeking similar books.

Thank you. I am grateful you have chosen to purchase this book and are taking the time to read it. You can find similar books available at:

www.wordsareswordspublishing.com.

Thank you,

- *Steven Matthews*

Who Was John McAfee?

John McAfee was many things to many people. Depending on who you asked, he would be portrayed as either a hero or supervillain.

For better or for worse, no one alive can rival the real-life adventures of John McAfee. Here are just a handful of strange-but-true McAfee facts included in this book:

- Was kicked out of college for having sex in public.
- As a college dropout, McAfee's first job was with NASA.
- Used psychedelics on a daily basis while working at prestigious companies for over a decade.
- Wrote the first anti-virus software in one day.
- Encouraged "sex, drugs, and hijinks" at his company after writing the very first computer anti-virus software in less than one day.
- Bought an island where he built 5 houses for his prostitutes.
- Faked a heart attack to escape police custody.

There is no question that McAfee lived a full life with no regrets. The world-renowned computer scientist, activist, business leader and cryptocurrency evangelist made himself a career that spans nearly the entire history of computing, all the while keeping his finger on the pulse of emerging technology.

McAfee was a master of writing his own press release and unrivaled when it came to appearing in the media. Throughout his entire adult life, not a month would go by that McAfee didn't appear in the headlines. This caused a myriad of stories and myths to engulf McAfee and those he surrounded himself with – even more than he intended.

Clearly, John loved building things. He loved creating value out of nothing – and he was good at it. One thing that he was never particularly good at was the daily grind. John couldn't handle the monotony. He was afraid of become stagnant. That becomes evident when looking back at his career and how he never seemed to hold a job for more than 2 years. In fact, every 2-3 years appears to be a new chapter in McAfee's life. Either he quit his job to find a new one or he would pack up and move somewhere else. With that in mind, it's safe to assume that McAfee's attention span only lasted 2-3 years.

His foray into the business world earn him friends in high places, but the misadventures in his personal life created numerous, powerful enemies, causing him to spend his last few years on the run and always looking over his shoulder.

In this biography, we will separate fact from fiction to discover who the true John McAfee really was while tell his story with no bias.

This is the real John McAfee.

Growing Up

John McAfee's youth would come to influence much of his life in later years, including one dark family secret which haunted him until his last breath.

Nothing about McAfee was what most people would regard as "normal", but least of all his birth. John David McAfee was born in the city of Cinderford, in the Forest of Dean, Gloucestershire on September 18, 1945. He was delivered on U.S. Army base in the United Kingdom because his father, Don McAfee, as a soldier stationed there at the time.

John McAfee's mother was a British girl local to the Army base in Cinderford who fell in love Don. Though he was born overseas, being delivered in a U.S. Army base made John an American citizen, although according to McAfee himself, he's "always felt as much British as American."

John was still very young when the family moved to Salem, Virginia, where he was raised. As McAfee recalls, there was nothing abnormal about his childhood and upbringing as a young boy growing up in the 1950's Virginia suburbs. The family had a white picket fence, large front yard that required regular mowing, and like many families in the 1950's, an abusive, alcoholic father.

John's Father Commits Suicide

John didn't think much about his father drinking all the time, coming home late, listening to his parent's arguments, or even the occasional beatings for him and his mother. He was strangely complacent with it at the time, as if this is just what normal families do. In an interview years later, John described his father as, "the negotiator of my mistrust."

But John's world view was shattered when he turned 15 and witnessed his father commit suicide with a gunshot to the head.

Although his mother never fully recovered from the suicide, John found his own way to cope with the sadness and started taking pills and smoking weed – all while never missing a day of school.

Being raised by a widowed mother was not easy for John. In addition to the emotional scarring left by his father's suicide, John and his mother struggled financially. John started his first job as a door-to-door magazine salesman while still in school to help support him and his mother.

Expelled from College for Sex in Public

Ever the diligent academic, John attended Roanoke College in Salem, Virginia, where he received a bachelor's degree in mathematics in 1967. While working on his PhD at Northeast Louisiana State College, McAfee was already well known for his wild, eccentric behavior and proclivity for drugs and sex. This led to him getting thrown out of college for having a series of very public sexual exploits with an undergraduate student who would later become his first wife.

The school would subsequently award McAfee with an honorary Sc.D. degree in 2008 because of his lifetime achievements.

Now a college dropout with a taste for the party scene, McAfee began looking for work, and if we know one thing about the world of John McAfee, as one door closes, another opens right up.

Space Cadet

Despite having a reputation as somewhat of a hedonist with a love for sex and drugs, McAfee had another reputation that would often proceed him before walking into a room for an interview:

Tech genius.

Fascinated by the primitive computers and emerging technology in the 70s, there was nothing McAfee loved more than tinkering with new gadgets. McAfee was a highly intelligent young man with an uncanny knack for programming. Because of his excellent skills and knowledge, he was able to get jobs in reputed organizations despite his drug addiction and alcoholism.

McAfee's first job after getting thrown out of college was working as a programmer with NASA's Institute for Space Studies in New York City in 1968. The job only lasted 2 years before he left NASA due to "irreconcilable differences".

It's no secret that McAfee was never a fan of the government or it's policies, but whether or not that belief played a role in his leaving NASA is unknown.

Psychedelics:
Micro-dosing and Macro-dosing

From New York, McAfee traveled to Missouri where he got a job working with the Missouri Pacific railroad in 1969. Coming from NASA to work on the railroad, John believed that the job was beneath him and would began to dabble with harder drugs. He would go to work many days while tripping on LSD. One day he was sold a bag of a psychedelic known as DMT. McAfee snorted a line of the drug, felt nothing, and then decided to do the whole bag. According to McAfee, "That's when I lost my mind."

After a life changing psychedelic experience where John claims to have, "went to the other side, walked amount spirits, and spoke with the gods," he was later found passed out behind a dumpster in downtown St. Luis.

For better or worse, McAfee would often revisit that fateful day and believed that it inadvertently changed his way of thinking for the rest of his life.

In 1977, when personal computers became commercially available around the country and with the release of the Apple Home Computer, McAfee made it his mission to learn everything he could about the device and how it works. As more and more companies were adopting computers and integrating them as a part of their businesses, there was a surge for the demand for computer scientists. Although John found the term "computer scientist" laughable, he eagerly accepted the opportunity to work with computers for a living and companies were paying very well for anyone with experience at the time.

Throughout his entire career, McAfee never had a hard time finding work. His skill and knowledge of computers and programming became highly sought after, leading to a series of short stints working with various tech giants. He would later work at Univac as a software designer before leaving to become an operating system architect at Xerox. In 1978, he joined Computer Sciences Corporation as a software consultant. He worked for consulting firm Booz Allen Hamilton from 1980 to 1982.

Throughout the 70s and 80s, McAfee remained a casual user of drugs and alcohol on a day-to-day basis, which could be one of the reasons he was unable to find stability in any job and generally quit or was fired after only two years at each company.

Falling into a deep depression in 1983, McAfee's drug use grew to new heights. He was working for Omex and was often found drinking and taking drugs in his office. His employers were very angry at his irresponsible behavior. According to McAfee, he would snort lines of coke underneath his desk first thing in the morning and polish off a bottle of scotch every day while living in constant fear that the drugs would run out. At this point, his wife left him, he gave away his dog, and he left his job working at Omex because of what he describes as "a mutual agreement."

McAfee spent days alone in his house doing nothing but drinking and drugs to numb his depression. He even admits that the idea of taking his own life, just as his father did, had crossed his mind.

McAfee had hit rock bottom. This was the wakeup call McAfee so desperately needed to sober up. He joined Alcoholics Anonymous and became sober for some time thereafter.

He was then employed by the famous defense contractor Lockheed Martin, where he worked on a classified voice-recognition program. It was here that he learned about a self-replicating code designed to copy itself on to any floppy disk inserted into affected computers.

The code was a virus called *Brain*, and from that moment on, his life would be forever changed.

The Anti-Virus Hustler

While developing software that could combat *Brain*, one of the first computer viruses in existence, something clicked inside of McAfee.

As he started developing software to combat viruses, he intuitively sensed that the menace of viruses would grow manifold in the coming years. People were terrified at the idea that their very expensive computers could be rendered useless hunks of metal by a virus. In this fear, McAfee saw an opportunity.

In 1987 McAfee founded McAfee Associates, an anti virus software company. According to McAfee, "My life didn't truly start until I started McAfee Associates."

By 1989, he had quit his job at Lockheed and devoted himself wholeheartedly to his fast-growing business. The threat of viruses increased worldwide and soon McAfee became a multi-million dollar business. During the mid-1990s, John McAfee sold off his stake in the business.

But McAfee Associates was not your typical software company and John was not a typical boss.

John was not the easiest person to work with, according to former McAfee employees who said that it was common for them to work for multiple days at a time while sleeping underneath their desks.

"If John was disappointed, he would let you know." Says an anonymous employee of McAfee's when the company first started out. "He was a free spirit, but he was also a bit of a perfectionist. He worked really, really hard. But I suppose we played hard, too.

During the first few years of the business, drugs, sex, and all sorts of hijinks were part of the company culture. Employees were encouraged to come to work in costumes and John would award people points for having sex in different places throughout the office.

Whatever they were doing at McAfee Associates was working. He was successful in a big way, beating out anti-virus competitors like Norton. But with that newfound success came more work for John.

The company was incorporated in Delaware in 1992, and McAfee resigned from the company in 1994. Two years after McAfee Associates went public, McAfee sold his remaining stake in the company for an estimated sum of $100 million.

Although he achieved his dreams of becoming a millionaire, McAfee would soon learn that with more money comes more problems.

The Eccentric Millionaire

If you're wondering why McAfee Anti-Virus software is already installed on the computer you just bought after John McAfee left his namesake company, you're not alone.

The McAfee Anti-Viral Saga is long and complicated. Network Associates was formed in 1997 as a merger of McAfee Associates and Network General. The Network Associates company name was retained for seven years, when it was renamed McAfee, Inc. In August 2010, Intel bought McAfee's company, maintaining the separate branding, until January 2014, when it announced that McAfee-related products will be marketed as Intel Security. McAfee expressed his pleasure at the name change, saying, "I am now everlastingly grateful to Intel for freeing me from this terrible association with the worst software on the planet." The unit was spun out of Intel in April 2017 as McAfee, LLC, as a joint venture between TPG Capital and Intel.

This consistent stream of revenue helped John start up a variety of new business ventures during the mid-90's and well into the turn of the century. He founded Tribal Voice, a company which developed the instant messaging program, PowWow, a company called Future Tense Central. In 2000, he invested in and joined the board of directors of Zone Labs, makers of firewall software, prior to its acquisition by Check Point Software in 2003. Rumor has it that McAfee started several other unsuccessful businesses around this time.

The Invention of Relaxation Yoga

Woodland Park was his home from 1994 to about 2002, so he lived there for about 8 years. Woodland Park was headquarters for his start-up company, Tribal Voice, until about 1999, when it was acquired by CMGI and then later it was his yoga center for the next 3 years.

Called the "The City Above the Clouds," Woodland Park, at 8,465 feet (2,580 m) above sea level, often enjoys clear skies while weather in neighboring towns may be rainy or overcast. The property included his 10,000-square-foot mansion perched on a hillside.

The home has five master bedrooms, a massive living room, den, large foyer, private theatre, library and fitness center. The master suite alone has a kitchen, fireplace, private entrance and floor to ceiling glass doors to the balcony that lead to a wood gazebo.

The property also has three different guest houses, two guest apartments and nine cabins. That's 19 bedrooms altogether. Also on the property are four trout lakes a massive observation deck, picnic tables, horse stables and more.

According to McAfee's personal contractor and handyman at the time, "He (John) is one of the nicest people you can ever meet in person. Very down to earth. The tub is one solid piece, which McAfee had imported from Europe. The walls are a Mayan pattern stone about 2" thick and this was his own design. He had the company create all the stones on the wall. The walls are also 10" thick concrete. The door to the master bedroom is on a center pivot with another nice pattern design on it. McAfee also added in-floor heating throughout, so anywhere you go in the house, it's warm on your feet. On a personal note, both John and I had a talk about the local art community which he enjoyed to visit the Business Of Art in Manitou Springs. John was, in my opinion, both smart and playful all his life from the talks we had."

In the early 2000's, John started teaching yoga classes from his Colorado mansion. In traditional John McAfee style, his yoga classes were ripe with casual sex and psychedelic drug use. He even sold videos of his yoga classes online at one point before getting hit with a law suit from one of his yoga students who appears in the video, naked and high.

As a yogi pioneer, McAfee invented a new form of yoga where he claimed that people could still get all of the health benefits of practicing yoga just by watching his yoga videos. He dubbed this practice, "relaxation yoga", and although there is no scientific explanation backing up these claims, it is still popular today.

In 2001, McAfee wrote and published 4 books on the subject of yoga, love, and spirituality, including *The Secret of the Yamas: Spiritual Guide to Yoga, The Fabric Of Self: Meditations on Vanity and Love, Into the Heart of Truth, Beyond the Siddhis: Supernatural Powers and the Sutras of Patanjali.*

McAfee would later discourage people from buying his books, claiming that they were all garbage. This form of reverse psychology seemed to dramatically increase his own book sales.

As a free spirit, John's penchant for casual sex landed him in hot water and lead to his second divorce, Judy McAfee, in 2002. John has always remained silent about Judy, and the nature of their relationship. It was a quiet divorce and the financial details are unknown.

Ultralights: Flying High

2002 was a pivotal year for John McAfee in many ways. He was tired of the yoga institute that he began in 2000, he had written several books, his business achievements were well recognized. John's net worth hit $100 million from his anti-virus business. McAfee and Associates was sold in 1997 for $7.6 billion. This is also the same year that he had received an honorary doctorate from his alma mater, Roanoke College.

2002 was also when John discovered ultralight flying. During a flight to Nepal, John saw an article in an inflight magazine about ultralights – basically a motorized hang glider. Hang gliders have no engine and are generally launched from high places and slowly descend. An ultralight glider, however, has a motor, so it can take off from anywhere and climb in altitude. Ultralight flying called to John's sense of adventure and remained a passion of his for the remainder of his life.

McAfee bought up massive stretches of land in Rodeo, New Mexico so the ultralights could make a long trip lasting several days by hopping from one base to another. The entire circuit he ended up building was 1,100 miles long. At each base, there would be some facilities for refueling and some basic human necessities. McAfee called it Sky Gypsies.

It was at this 157-acre complex where an accident killed two people – the ultralight pilot and McAfee's 22-year-old nephew, Joel Bitow, and his passenger, Robert Gilson, on Nov 1, 2006.

McAfee brushed off the incident, reminding the media to, "keep in mind that every adventure sport has it's own risks. The issue is whether you can manage them or not. When we were aerotrekking, we were always riding the line between safety and danger."

The crash was believed to be the result of Joel Bitlow's inexperience as a pilot coupled with him attempting some advanced ultralight maneuvers during unsafe flying conditions. However, the accidental deaths of two ultralight fliers would ultimately result in a $5 million lawsuit and McAfee's departure from the United States.

Although McAfee predicted the coming financial crash in 2006, he still lost a lot of money. According to a report published in August 2009 in The New York Times, McAfee's personal fortune had declined to $4 million from $100 million due to Great Recession between 2007 to 2008.

It's estimated that John's financial loss was recuperated by investing in Bitcoin and other cryptocurrencies around this time, however, he has never confirmed nor denied the volume of his digital assets.

From 2004 to 2007, John McAfee sold off 4 properties, including a 1,044-acre oceanfront plantation in Hawaii for $3.13 million, a villa in Port Isabel, Texas for $2.2 million, an oceanfront estate in Molokai for $1.7 million, and finally his Colorado estate in Woodland Park for $5.72 million.

Thus, he did cash in before the crash in the real estate market in 2008. McAfee had all of these properties sold in an auction, so he likely took a considerable loss on them in order to get liquid capital quickly. The property in New Mexico was sold after the real estate market crash.

After making his fortune in technology and losing most of it in the housing market crash, John was ready to adopt a low profile. However, keeping a low profile is not something he was particularly good at.

The King of the Jungle

In the wake of several lawsuits brought against McAfee and his companies totaling over $5 million, coupled with the rapidly growing regulatory industries within the United States and John's ultimate mistrust of them, he sold off his all off all of his properties, liquidated his physical assets, and bought a small, private island in the country of Belize.

History has shown us that what John McAfee loved most is building and scaling businesses. A look at some of the entrepreneurial endeavors McAfee started in the 2000s reveals that many of his business aspirations were tapered by the U.S. legal system and regulatory departments. Being an outspoken libertarian and proponent of both personal and business freedom, the relaxed law and regulatory bodies in Belize made the small country an obvious choice John.

The Infamous Belize Years

John McAfee's adventures in the jungles of Belize are well-documented in the 2018 documentary produced by Showtime, *Gringo: The Dangerous Life of John McAfee*, however, the film has since been discredited by a series of contradictory narratives made by most, if not all of the witnesses interviewed. Both the director of *Gringo* and McAfee's former employees who once worked for him during his time in Belize have since rescinded their statements and accusations, stating that they were paid by *Gringo* director Nanette Burstein to make inflammatory statements on camera. Burstein's responded to these accusations by pointing the finger at McAfee himself, claiming that he must have paid his former Belizian employees to accuse her of bribing them.

McAfee claimed that these incidents were fabricated, saying that "Belize is a third-world banana republic and you can go down there and make any story you want if you pay your interviewees, which Showtime did."

This has created a sense of mythology surrounding McAfee, and while we may never know the truth, Here is what we know for sure about John McAfee's time spent in Belize:

> ➤ We know that John built a sprawling compound in Belize in 2010, including a laboratory for research.

> ➤ McAfee started the company QuorumEx from his Belize estate, which aimed to produce herbal

antibiotics that disrupt quorum sensing in bacteria.

➤ McAfee has a growing impact on Belize's economy. As his company grows, so does the number of local jobs available.

➤ John routinely made donations to the Belize community, including the local police department, for whom he purchased bullet-proof vests, tasers, tear gas, and a boat.

➤ By all accounts, McAfee also became more paranoid around this time and dramatically increased the number of personal armed guards surrounding him at all times.

➤ McAfee was known for taking in stray dogs wandering the city streets. At one point, he had at least 4 stray dogs that he fed and housed at his complex.

➤ Even in Belize, John was as hyper-sexual as ever. He was well-known with local sex workers and would later build five different bungalows on his property for his favorite "girlfriends."

Back in 2012, despite being surrounded by quite a nice flock of young women and two homes in Belize, not all was blissful in the paradise he manufactured. He seemed to enjoy the attention given to the fact he shared his homes with a number of lovely young local women, many of whom described McAfee's sexual appetite as insatiable.

Many have wondered about the goings-ons in those dark days of Belize, but when he isn't trying to make headlines on his own terms, John McAfee is a pretty private person. Unfortunately, his penchant for privacy coupled with the abundance of armed guards he surrounded himself with started to arouse the suspicion of the government in Belize.

On April 30, 2012, McAfee's property in Orange Walk Town, Belize, was raided by the Gang Suppression Unit of the Belize Police Department. At that time, McAfee was in bed with a girlfriend. A GSU press release stated that McAfee was arrested for unlicensed drug manufacturing and possession of an unlicensed weapon. The police found an abundance of white powder throughout McAfee's laboratory, but it did not test positive for narcotics. He was later released without charges.

In 2012, Belize police spokesman, Raphael Martinez, confirmed that McAfee was neither convicted nor charged, only suspected.

McAfee insists that the event was a violation of his right to privacy, likening the raid to that of an unruly mob gathering outside Frankenstein's castle, only instead of pitchforks and torches they carried bullet proof vests and automatic weapons.

The Murder of Gregory Faull

On November 11, 2012, John McAfee's neighbor, Greg Faull, was found dead in his house. His killers have never been found. Greg was shot to death in the house that he designed and built in Belize. Greg had come to Belize after the hurricane, and felt he found the perfect place to build his dream home.

Greg seemed the direct opposite of John McAfee in many ways. While McAfee was involved in a dozen projects, Greg was relaxing and fishing. They did not get along. John McAfee's dogs were stray dogs, and a menace to people walking on the beach. John McAfee had late night parties, and taxis would be arriving late into the night. The noise bothered Greg and he complained to the police. We learned later that before Greg moved in to the house, he rented it to John McAfee, who was in the initial stages of setting up a laboratory, to produce anti-bacterial medicines based on through a relatively new research in biology "quorum sensing."

Until Greg's murder is solved, a cloud of suspicion will hang over McAfee's head, although there has been no evidence to date to directly connect him to the crime other than speculative testimony. He has never been a prime suspect in the crime, only a "person of interest" and Belize police want to question him.

Everyone waited patiently for the next shoe to drop on Greg Faull's murder. There was nothing from the police. There were many unanswered questions. It appears there was no forced entry. Greg was shot with a 9 mm Lugar pistol in the upstairs of his house. He was murdered at night after his walk from his favorite bar. From what little evidence there was, it seems Greg knew his killers. He was a very big, strong man. From this, it seems realistic he was killed in his home.

Unfortunately, because the local police in Belize lack even rudimentary forensic equipment, such as the ability to test for fingerprints, and DNA, it is unlikely that this case will ever be solved.

He said that he has always been afraid police in Belize would kill him, and thus refused their routine questions; he has since evaded the Belizean authorities. Belize's prime minister, Dean Barrow, called McAfee "extremely paranoid, even bonkers." McAfee fled Belize when he was sought for questioning concerning the murder.

John remains adamant that he is innocent in the Greg Faull case. Rather than prove his innocents and go through the system in a country that is ripe with corruption, McAfee chose to play by his own rules, as he always has.

John fled Belize in a hurry, leaving behind his estate and all of his possessions except for what he could carry. In January 2014, McAfee claimed that when the Belizean government raided his property, it seized his assets, and that his house later burned down under suspicious circumstances.

Faking a Heart Attack & Deportation

With a long history of non-compliance with governments and authorities, John left Belize across the Guatemala border where he stayed at a hotel in a rural town.

While staying at the hotel in Guatemala, John is in communication with Vice. John tells Vice that he would like to tell them his side of the story and agrees to an interview. However, when the Vice camera crew arrives in Guatemala, John is arrested by Interpol during the interview.

The magazine Vice accidentally gave away McAfee's location at a Guatemalan resort in early December 2012, when a photo taken by one of its journalists accompanying McAfee was posted with the EXIF geolocation metadata still attached. While in Guatemala, McAfee asked Chad Essley, an American cartoonist and animator, to set up a blog so that McAfee could write about his experience while on the run. McAfee then appeared publicly in Guatemala City, where he attempted to seek political asylum.

On December 5, 2012, McAfee was arrested for illegally entering Guatemala. Shortly afterward, he was placed under arrest, and a board to review McAfee's plea for asylum was formed. The committee denied his asylum, so he was taken from his holding facility to a detention center in order to await deportation to Belize.

On December 6, 2012, Reuters and ABC News reported that McAfee had two minor heart attacks in a Guatemalan detention center and was hospitalized.

McAfee's lawyer stated that his client had not suffered heart attacks, but had instead suffered from high blood pressure and anxiety attacks. McAfee later said he had faked the heart attacks while being held in Guatemala, to buy time for his attorney to file a series of appeals that ultimately prevented his deportation to Belize, thus hastening the government's decision to send him back to the United States.

On December 12, 2012, McAfee was released from detention in Guatemala, and deported to the Florida.

The Cryptocurrency Guru

The night after McAfee arrived in the United States after being deported from Guatemala in December 2012, John was sitting at a bar in Miami Beach planning his next move. Seeing John drinking alone at the bar with a somber look on his face, a beautiful, young African American woman approaches John as asks him if he wants a blow job.

"You look like you could use it." Said Janice Dyson, then a prostitute in Miami Beach. "Those were my first words to John."

The two spent the night together. Despite Dyson being more than 30 years younger than John, the two started dating and before long they got married in 2013.

Back in the states and without a plan, McAfee moved to Portland, Oregon, in 2013.

By then, McAfee is back on American soil and back in the tech world. He announces his new latest company – Future Tense Central – and his latest invention – D-Central – a portable, wireless mini-router that can fit in one's pocket while creating a personal mini-internet. With the announcement, McAfee is once again making headlines, both good and bad, although he has no trouble finding investors for his new start-up.

Years later, McAfee and his business partners would pivot D-Central to become a decentralized bitcoin mining tool.

John had many interests, but at this point in his life, he began to lean in hard on two things: cryptocurrency and privacy. Here are a few of the headlines he made during these years:

> ➤ At the DEF CON conference in Las Vegas, Nevada, in August 2014, he warned Americans not to use smartphones, suggesting apps are used to spy on clueless consumers who do not read privacy user agreements.

> ➤ In February 2016, McAfee received media attention by publicly volunteering to decrypt the iPhone used by the San Bernardino shooters, avoiding the need for Apple to build a backdoor. McAfee later admitted that his claims of how simple cracking the phone would be were a publicity stunt, though he still claimed he could pull it off.

> ➤ In July 2017, McAfee wrote on Twitter that he predicted that the price of one bitcoin would jump to $500,000 within three years, and "If not, I will eat my own dick on national television." In July 2019, he continued to defend a prediction of $1 million by the end of 2020. In January 2020, however, he stated on Twitter that his previous predictions were simply "A ruse to onboard new users", and that bitcoin had limited potential because it was "an ancient technology".

- In May 2016, McAfee was appointed chief executive chairman and CEO of MGT Capital Investments, a technology holding company. The company initially stated that it would rename itself John McAfee Global Technologies, although this plan was abandoned due to a dispute with Intel over rights to the "McAfee" name. McAfee changed MGT's focus from social gaming to cybersecurity, stating in an interview that "anti-virus software is dead, it no longer works," and that "the new paradigm has to stop the hacker getting in" before they can do damage.

- Soon after joining MGT, McAfee claimed that he and his team had exploited a flaw in the Android operating system that allowed him to read encrypted messages from WhatsApp. Gizmodo investigated these claims, and reported that McAfee had sent reporters malware-infected phones to make this hack work. McAfee responded to these accusations, writing: "Of course the phones had malware on them. How that malware got there is the story, which we will release after speaking with Google. It involves a serious flaw in the Android architecture."

- McAfee moved MGT into the mining of bitcoin and other cryptocurrencies, saying that it was intended both to make money for the company, and to increase MGT's expertise in dealing with blockchains, which he thought was important for cybersecurity.

- ➤ In August 2017, McAfee stepped down as CEO, instead serving as MGT's "chief cybersecurity visionary." In January 2018, he left the company altogether. Both sides stated that the decision was amicable, with McAfee saying that he wanted to spend all of his time on cryptocurrencies, while the company stated that they were getting pressured by potential investors to disassociate themselves from McAfee.

- ➤ On August 13, 2018, McAfee took a position of CEO with Luxcore, a cryptocurrency company focused on enterprise solutions.

- ➤ McAfee has always had a sense of humor about his work and never takes himself too seriously. A perfect example is this hilarious viral video he made with instruction on how to remove McAfee Anti-Virus from your computer: https://youtu.be/bKgf5PaBzyg

For years, John made his fortune as a cryptocurrency guru, once again using his expertise with technology to make a name for himself, but major news headline weren't enough for John. Fed up with the rampant regulations he encountered while scaling his business, McAfee decided it was time to run for president of the United States.

Presidential Campaign

In September 2015, John McAfee announced that he would run for the office of U.S. President in the 2016 presidential election as a member of the newly-formed Cyber Party. Then, on December 24, 2015, he re-announced his candidacy bid saying that he would instead seek the presidential nomination of the Libertarian Party.

McAfee ran on a libertarian platform, advocating the decriminalization of cannabis, an end to the war on drugs, non-interventionism in foreign policy, a free market economy which does not redistribute wealth, and upholding free trade. McAfee supported abolishing the Transportation Security Administration.

On the issues, McAfee advocated increased cyber awareness, and more action against the threat of cyberwarfare and advocated religious liberty, saying that business owners should be able to deny service in circumstances that contradict their religious beliefs, and: "No one is forcing you to buy anything. No one is forcing you to choose one person over another. Why should I be forced to do anything if I'm not harming anyone? It's my choice to sell, just as it's your choice to buy."

On the campaign trail, McAfee consistently polled among the top three presidential candidates for his party with his rivals Gary Johnson and Austin Petersen. The three candidates appeared in the Libertarian Party's first nationally televised presidential debate on March 29,

2016. John would later run his presidential campaign on a yacht in international waters.

McAfee announced that his vice-presidential choice would be the photographer, former commercial real estate broker, and Libertarian activist Judd Weiss. During his 2016 presidential campaign, John had several notable endorsements, including talk show host and activist, Adam Kokesh, Nevada assemblyman, John Moore, and science fiction author and activist, Neil Smith.

McAfee was the runner-up in the primaries, but came in third at the 2016 Libertarian National Convention.

2020 Presidential Campaign

Contrary to his assertion at the 2016 convention, McAfee announced on June 3, 2018, via Twitter that he would run for president again in 2020, either with the Libertarian Party or under the banner of a party of his own creation. His main campaign issue was to promote the use of cryptocurrencies. He stated that he will either again seek the nomination of the Libertarian Party, or form his own party; he ultimately ran as a Libertarian.

On January 22, 2019, McAfee announced via Twitter that he would be continuing his campaign "in exile", following reports that he, his wife, and four of his campaign staff were being indicted for tax-related felonies by the IRS. McAfee indicated that he was in "international waters", and had previously tweeted that he was on his way to Venezuela.

The IRS has not commented on the alleged indictments. On June 29, McAfee tweeted that his campaign headquarters had been relocated to Havana, Cuba.

Around the same time, McAfee defended Communist revolutionary Che Guevara on Twitter, putting himself at odds with the Libertarian Party, with Libertarian National Committee chairman Nicholas Sarwark saying, "I hear very little buzz about McAfee this time around ... making a defense of Che Guevara from Cuba may ingratiate him with the Cuban government, but it didn't resonate well with Libertarians."

In a tweet, on March 4, 2020, McAfee simultaneously suspended his 2020 presidential campaign and announced his campaign for the Libertarian party vice presidential nomination. The next day, he returned to the presidential field, reversing the suspension of his bid, as "No one in the Libertarian Party Would consider me For Vice President."

The next month, he endorsed Adam Kokesh; he simultaneously became Kokesh's vice-presidential candidate, though McAfee decided to also continue his campaign for the presidency. McAfee was again not nominated, losing to Jo Jorgensen and Spike Cohen for the vice-presidential slot.

International Fugitive

After a failed presidential campaign, John McAfee spent the final years of his life on the run from the law.

On August 2, 2015, McAfee was arrested in Henderson County, Tennessee, on one count of driving under the influence and one count of possession of a firearm while intoxicated.

On November 14, 2018, the Circuit Court in Orlando, Florida, refused to dismiss a wrongful death lawsuit against McAfee for Faull's death.

In January 2019, McAfee announced that he was on the run from U.S. authorities, and living internationally on a boat following the convening of a Grand Jury to indict him, his wife, and four of his 2020 Presidential campaign workers on tax-related charges. As on 2021, the IRS has not confirmed or denied the existence of these charges.

In July 2019, McAfee and members of his entourage were arrested while his yacht was docked at Puerto Plata, Dominican Republic, on suspicion of carrying high-caliber weapons and ammunition. They were held for four days before being released.

On August 11, 2020, McAfee fabricated a hoax that he was arrested in Norway during the COVID-19 pandemic, after refusing to replace a lace thong with a more effective face mask. McAfee later posted a picture of himself to Twitter with a bruised eye, claiming that it occurred during this arrest. However, the photo of the alleged arrest shows an officer with the German word for "police" on their uniform, so it could not have been an arrest in Norway. The Augsburg Police later confirmed McAfee unsuccessfully attempted to enter Germany on that day, but was not arrested.

On October 5, 2020, McAfee was arrested in Spain at the request of the U.S. Department of Justice for tax evasion. The indictment alleges he earned millions of dollars from 2014–18, but has failed to file income tax returns.

On October 6, 2020, the U.S. Securities and Exchange Commission filed a complaint alleging that McAfee had fraudulently promoted certain ICOs. According to the SEC, McAfee presented himself as an impartial investor when he promoted the ICOs, despite the fact that he was allegedly paid $23 million in digital assets in exchange for the promotions.

Death and Taxes

McAfee contended that taxes are illegal and claimed in 2019 that he had not filed a tax return since 2010. He referred to himself as being a "prime target" of the U.S. Internal Revenue Service.

On March 5, 2021, the U.S. Attorney's Office for the Southern District of New York announced that they had formally indicted McAfee and an executive adviser for allegedly fraudulently promoting certain cryptocurrencies and performing pump and dump schemes. McAfee was incarcerated in Spain, pending extradition to the United States.

On June 23, 2021, McAfee was found dead in his Barcelona prison cell in Brians 2 Penitentiary, hours after the Spanish National Court approved of his extradition to the United States on tax evasion charges. The Catalan Justice Department said in a statement that "everything indicates" McAfee took his own life.

Though John McAfee may no longer be with us, his legacy lives on through his inventions, software, companies, and of course, his immortal words of wisdom/ While awaiting extradition in a Spanish prison, McAfee continued to tweet out hilarious, ominous, and often insightful messages.

Read some of the many outlandish McAfee-isms in the next chapter of this book.

In Loving Memory of John McAfee,

An American Hustler.

The Best of McAfee Quotes

John McAfee was well known for speaking his mind – as shocking,

Even though his words would often land him in trouble, he

These are the best of McAfee-isms.

"Getting subtle messages from U.S. officials saying, in effect: 'We're coming for you McAfee! We're going to kill yourself". I got a tattoo today just in case. If I suicide myself, I didn't. I was whacked."

(On Twitter, December 1, 2019)

"A good example is more irritating than a bad one."

(From a presentation in Munich, Jan 1991, in response to an audience question on why his competitors complained about his business practices.)

*"If you own the facts, you may
distort them as you like."*

(To anti-virus researcher Pame Kane at the 1992 Computer Virus Conference in response to Kane's assertion that McAfee's virus scanner did not work.)

*"Ignorance and confidence are
constant companions."*

(Into the Heart of Truth, 2001)

*"Disobedience is the vehicle of
progress."*

(Explaining why he did not follow the normal rules of business to reporter Josh Quittner in 1992.)

*"History is sympathetic to its
authors."*

(Into the Heart of Truth, 2001)

*"If the majority holds something of
value, you can be certain it has none."*

(Anti-virus presentation, Sydney Australia, 1991, on the general trend away from virus scanning as a valid method of virus control.)

"Opinions need a willing ear."

(Beyond the Sindhis, 2002)

*"If you have the winning cards,
why cheat?"*

(Good Morning America (June 1991) when asked if he manipulated the results of his product's virus detection percentage.)

"Hope is paltry food for living."

(Into the Heart of Truth, 2001)

*"Software production is unlike any
other production that preceded it. No
raw materials are required, no time is
required, and no effort is required.
You can make a million copies of a
piece of software instantaneously for
free. It's a totally new paradigm of
production."*

("Nerds 2.0.1 - A Brief History of the Internet", Part 3)

*"I think that it's when we step out
of the road, step outside the box,
become our own person and we walk
fearlessly down paths other people
wouldn't look at, that true progress
comes. And sometimes true beauty as
well."*

(BBC News: "John McAfee: Addict, coder, runaway", 2013)

*"I am not implying that our entire
Government is corrupt. I am saying
that it is corrupt to the point that no-
one is untouched by it."*

(On Twitter, June 10 2019)

*"I am content in here. I have
friends. The food is good. All is well.
Know that if I hang myself, a la
Epstein, it will be no fault of mine."*

(On Twitter, October 16, 2020)

*"There is much sorrow in prison,
disguised as hostility."*

(On Twitter just days before his death)

*"The sorrow is plainly visible even
in the most angry faces."*

(On Twitter just days before his death)

*"I'm old and content with food and
a bed but for the young prison is a
horror - a reflection of the minds of
those who conceived them."*

(On Twitter, June 10, 2021. 2 weeks before his death)

*"Now its Jeff Bezos.
If space travel improves and becomes
fashionable perhaps we can abandon
the planet we have so thoroughly
mangled and seek fresh ones to trash."*

(On Twitter, June 8, 2021)

*"The ones who are crazy enough to
think that they can change the world
are the ones who do."*

(On Twitter, date unknown)

"This new business paradigm empowers individuals to better shape their own destiny and leverage their existing assets to their benefit."

(On Twitter, date unknown)

"Making money is easy. It is. "The difficult thing in life is not making it, it's keeping it."

(On Twitter, date unknown)

"Social engineering has become about 75% of an average hacker's toolkit, and for the most successful hackers, it reaches 90% or more."

(On Twitter, date unknown)

"Any idiot can make money. Keeping money, very few can do."

(On Twitter, date unknown)

"Our mobile phones have become the greatest spy on the planet."

(On Twitter, date unknown)

"The most astonishing subset of the Deep Web is a collection of dark alleys called the Dark Web. The Dark Web is generally thought of as a collection of criminal elements intent on subverting the law, stealing our money, and possibly kidnapping our daughters."

(On Twitter, date unknown)

"In this age of communications that span both distance and time, the only tool we have that approximates a 'whisper' is encryption. When I cannot whisper in my wife's ear or the ears of my business partners, and have to communicate electronically, then encryption is our tool to keep our secrets secret."

(On Twitter, date unknown)

"Governments are composed of human beings, and all of the frailties that humans possess are absorbed into these governments and become active within these governments. Hatred, anger, jealousy, fear, greed, distrust and the whole host of afflictions that humans must bear, lurk just beneath the surface of civility displayed by 'government.'"

(On Twitter, date unknown)

"Hackers rarely have full knowledge of the technology stack of a target."

(On Twitter, date unknown)

"I was one of the first practitioners of social engineering as a hacking technique, and today it is my only tool of use, aside from a smartphone - in a purely white hat sort of way. But if you don't trust me, then ask any reasonably competent social engineer."

(On Twitter, date unknown)

"My most heartfelt thank you goes to Impact Future Media and Cartoon Monkey Studio. Their dedication to the truth is very uncommon in the world we live in today. I am now, and will always be, grateful to their organizations."

(On Twitter, date unknown)

"Let me tell you what the truth is... I have learned one thing in life: there is no such thing as bad press. There is not. That's a fundamental truth. The more bad things said about you, the more power they give to you."

(On Twitter, date unknown)

"Jealousy, greed, fear. We're all full of these things. But also love and compassion. If you saw a drowning baby, it wouldn't matter if you were wearing a tuxedo on the way to your own wedding. You'd jump in to save him."

(On Twitter, date unknown)

"When a hacker gains access to any corporate data, the value of that data depends on which server, or sometimes a single person's computer, that the hacker gains access to."

(On Twitter, date unknown)

"Sometimes private communication systems have been around since the beginning of human culture."

(On Twitter, date unknown)

"Limit use of shareware and public domain software to systems without fixed disks. If you do use them on fixed disks, allocate separate subdirectories... Public domain or shareware software should never be placed in the root directory. "

(On Twitter, date unknown)

"I, perhaps wrongly, assume that people actually read articles that interest them rather than just headlines."

(On Twitter, date unknown)

"My fragile connection with the world of polite society has, without a doubt, been severed."

(On Twitter, date unknown)

"My well-discussed 'paranoia' urges me to believe that some tiny segment of the NSA's parsing algorithm is finely tuned to my voice."

(On Twitter, date unknown)

"Is Snowden a good man or a bad man? I have no clue and even less interest."

(On Twitter, date unknown)

"These 'free' applications ask for permission to read your emails, your text messages, listen to your phone calls, record video from your phone. Why else would someone spend millions developing an application which they then give away? ("John McAfee Quotes - BrainyQuote") Kind-hearted, maybe? Get real."

(On Twitter, date unknown)

"I think that it's when we step out of the road, step outside the box, become our own person, and we walk fearlessly down paths other people wouldn't look at, that true progress comes. And sometimes true beauty as well."

(On Twitter, date unknown)

"The FBI and our entire government has become a bureaucracy. Sick, tired, and old as far as technology is concerned. This has to change."

(On Twitter, date unknown)

"There's not a single flashlight app that's not spying on you right now."

(On Twitter, date unknown)

"Every corporation worth its salt is throwing money at Deep Web research, not least Google. The company that unlocks the mysteries of the Deep Web will obtain power of an enormous magnitude."

(On Twitter, date unknown)

"I was an altar boy. I could probably quote the Bible from beginning to end."

(On Twitter, date unknown)

"If operating in a network environment, do not place public domain or shareware programs in a common file-server directory that could be accessible to any other PC on the network."

(On Twitter, date unknown)

"When we do not understand something, a common reaction is to fear it. In government, this is the usual, and encouraged, reaction. The reaction to the gig economy has been no different, and this growing fear has unfortunately turned into a legislative bloodbath."

(On Twitter, date unknown)

"Libertarian principles are very simple, but you can't violate any of them and still call yourself a Libertarian."

(On Twitter, date unknown)

"Steve Jobs would have wanted his words to change not just technology but politics itself."

(On Twitter, date unknown)

*"One who understands the
relationships between the human
heart and the human mind will always
out-hack those who chase after an
ever-changing technology."*

(On Twitter, date unknown)

*"The world chooses to think what
the world thinks."*

(On Twitter, date unknown)

*"When individuals become angry
with one another, an injury of some
sort will likely occur. When
governments become angry, entire
civilisations are wiped out."*

(On Twitter, date unknown)

*"The most promising privacy thing
is stupid phones. I'm dumping all my
smart phones."*

(On Twitter, date unknown)

"I would like to point to the extraordinary lengths the mainstream media will go to maintain a sensationalist story."

(On Twitter, date unknown)

"I think that the world has largely ignored Belize and the political situation and the plight of its people because it's one of the smallest countries and, in terms of the world economy, one of the least significant."

(On Twitter, date unknown)

"When you're standing in line at the airport, and your shoes are off, your belt is off, and your personal belongings are being closely scrutinized, and you're standing with your hands in the air, waiting to be patted down, do you feel protected? I don't. I feel like I'm the enemy."

(On Twitter, date unknown)

"People are afraid of their own lives. Shouldn't your goal be to have a meaningful life? Unknown, mysterious, thrilling?"

(On Twitter, date unknown)

"A hacker is someone who uses a combination of high-tech cybertools and social engineering to gain illicit access to someone else's data. That is all."

(On Twitter, date unknown)

"We are losing privacy at an alarming rate - we have none left."

(On Twitter, date unknown)

"Every newspaper on earth has called me a liar. I simply would like to live comfortably day by day, fish, swim, enjoy my declining years."

(On Twitter, date unknown)

"Really, what the government is asking Apple to do is to make every individual who uses an iPhone susceptible to hacking by bad people, foreign governments, and anyone who wants."

(On Twitter, date unknown)

"Politicon [political convention] should be applauded for recognizing the increasing impact of technology, not only on American social and economic systems but on the very structure of our system of politics."

(On Twitter, date unknown)

"Belize is so raw and so clear and so in-your-face. "There's an opportunity to see something about human nature that you can't really see in a politer society, because the purpose of society is to mask ourselves from each other."

(On Twitter, date unknown)

"Corporate competition is fierce, viewed by many as economic warfare where all is fair. But politics... now, this is something unique."

(On Twitter, date unknown)

"We as Americans have ripped off the world. We get to throw food away. It's insane."

(On Twitter, date unknown)

"There is dissatisfaction in all of us. Some of us take out that dissatisfaction by attempting to ruin whatever you are attempting to do. This is a fact of life. "

(On Twitter, date unknown)

John McAfee's Resume

(Just for fun, this is an actual resume John McAfee used circa 2012)

Education

BS Mathematics, Roanoke College, West Virginia, 1968

Experience

Computer Programmer/Systems Analyst:

(1969 – 1987):   Worked at various companies, beginning with NASA in New York City (1969), worked at Xerox, Computer Science Corporation and Lockheed.

Founder/President:

(1987 – 1994) McAfee and Associates, Created the first company to offer anti-virus software to the public. Company went public in 1992.   Although the company was a huge success, I left in 1994 to pursue other interests.

Founder/President:

(1994 – 1999) Tribal Voice, Woodland Park.

I developed first internet instant messaging service and sold the company to CMGI

Owner:

(1999 – 2002) Yoga School, Woodland Park, Colorado.

Author of several yoga books, producer of video on yoga.

Owner:

(2002 – 2007) Sky Gypsies, New Mexico.

Providing ultra-light flight school, aerotreking and community center with lodging, restaurant and movie theater.

Owner/ investor:

2008 to 2012: Various projects in Belize including water sports store, water taxi service, ultra-light flight school.

Joint Owner/ President:

Ex-Quorum involved in research of natural antibiotics that would disrupt bacteria's quorum sensing capabilities. Laboratory located in Carmelita, Belize. Closed in 2010.

Ongoing Project:

Promotion of a graphic novel by Chad Essley (in preparation), film documentary and book on my life in collaboration with Image Future Media.

Personal

67-years-old (born September 18, 1945)

Presently single.

Hobbies

Piano, jet skiing, ultra-light flying.

Books Written by John McAfee

Computer Viruses, Worms, Data Diddlers, Killer Programs, and Other Threats to Your System. What They Are, How They Work, and how to Defend Your PC, Mac, Or Mainframe, St. Martin's Press, (1989)

The Secret of the Yamas. Spiritual Guide to Yoga, McAfee Pub, (2001)

The Fabric Of Self: Meditations on Vanity and Love, Woodland Publications, (2001)

Into the Heart of Truth, Woodland Publications, (2001)

Beyond the Siddhis. Supernatural Powers and the Sutras of Patanjali, Woodland Publications, (2001)

Recommended Reading

Other books by Steven Matthews in the 90-minute Biography series.

Scan the QR code to buy the book.

Nadia Comaneci - A Pioneer in Perfection

The True Story of Nadia Comaneci: An Inspirational Sports Story for Girls Just Getting into Sports, Gymnastics, Olympics.

Jon Stewart

How Jon Stewart Went from Making Political Jokes to Changing the World.

A Very Stephen Colbert Biography

How Steven Colbert went from Fake News to Real Comedy.

Learning from Steve Jobs

His Inventions, His Principles, His Life & Finding Innovation in an Age that Needs It Most.

www.ingramcontent.com/pod-product-compliance
Lightning Source LLC
Chambersburg PA
CBHW061432050726
47593CB00006B/2323